HOW TO SETTLE DEBTS WITH CREDITORS

A Bankruptcy Association Guide

John McQueen

The Bankruptcy Association

THIS BOOK IS A PUBLICATION OF
The Bankruptcy Association

4 Johnson Close
Abraham Heights
Lancaster
Lancashire
LA1 5EU
United Kingdom
Tel: (01524) 64305
Fax: (01524) 389717

First edition: April 2002

Conditions of Sale

Great efforts have been made by the Publisher and Author to ensure
that the information contained in this book is accurate. Information
can become out of date, however, and errors can creep in because of
author's and printer's errors. This book is sold, therefore, on the
condition that neither the Author nor Publisher can be held legally
responsible for the consequence of any error or omission there may
be.

ISBN 0 9518636 3 0

Printed in Great Britain by
The Bankruptcy Association

If you lived in the richest, most powerful city it was possible for a man to imagine, but there was no love there, no mercy and no justice for those who met with misfortune; then you would be better off dead than to live in such a place.

Contents

FOREWORD

I founded the Bankruptcy Association during March 1983. Since then I have spent most of my time living and breathing bankruptcy law and surrounding issues. During this period I have advised at least 20,000 individuals on their bankruptcy problems. Currently I am advising about 1,500 bankrupt people each year.

This is a short but I hope a thorough and accurate guide to enable readers to settle their debt problems with their creditors. It is impossible in any book, of any length, to deal with all the nuances and particular circumstances that surround each individual. Such a book, if it could be written, would be unreadable and unusable.

In this book therefore, I have adopted a policy of offering a simple, clear and repetitive method of dealing with creditors. The system described in this book, adapted to meet individual circumstances, works. It is the system that the Bankruptcy Association has applied very successfully in literally thousands of cases over nearly twenty years.

Many people have avoided the indignities involved in personal bankruptcy by following this advice. The proven avenues described in this book work, day in and day out, for anyone willing to follow them.

John McQueen
Lancaster
April 2002

1

Introduction

There are a myriad of reasons why millions of basically honest and decent British people find themselves saddled with serious debt problems. Business failures, divorces and low wages are just a few of the causes. This book is designed for people with serious personal or business debt problems. Its aims are to demystify debt issues and to offer a path towards a solution.

Serious debt can and quite often does psychologically overwhelm some people. Most people at some time or other have had some form of money worries. Occasionally the stress and worry of debt problems can make people ill. Often too, they are unable to think straight.

Money is a much sort after commodity. Creditors get upset and angry if people who owe them money do not pay them. They will retaliate by taking various actions to try to recover that money. This is when the distress starts, as creditors begin to apply pressure for repayment.

This is a brutal process that is based on the principles that govern debt and as such it takes no account of individual sensitivities. Well educated, highly competent people can be made to feel extremely humiliated by the processes creditors use to recover money. It is a fact that debt collectors use this fear and ignorance of the system to force payment ahead of other creditors.

Therefore the important concept that is vital for readers to understand is the paramount need to face the financial facts of their dilemma in as cool and dispassionate a manner as possible. However large the money worries are of any individual, one afternoon each month spent calmly facing up to their dilemma is all that is often required to solve even the most difficult financial problems.

2

The Basics of Debt

In general, there are two broad types of debtors. A consumer debtor is anyone, not in business, who has run up debts. This definition includes literally millions of people in the United Kingdom. The types of debt people face are many and varied ranging from mortgage and rent arrears, credit card debts, bank loans through to student loans.

There are many reasons for people running up these types of debts, not least of which is the ease with which credit can be obtained in today's society. It is much more difficult and in some cases impossible for people to cope with the debt repayments and eventually to climb out of debt.

A business debtor is someone running a business who has run up debts. Business debtors often face more complex debt problems because of the variety of creditors often involved. Business debtors will commonly be faced with special types of debt such as tax debts and business rates.

Many business debtors these days can often also be classified as consumer debtors as well, in that they have run up credit card debts in the same way as the more common consumer debtors.

Whatever types of debt a person has, the method of dealing with the debt problem is exactly the same. The only difference between the two is that they are likely to have different priority debts to pay.

How do we recognise the problem?

Before going further we need to consider when it is that an individual can be considered to be insolvent. This can be easily explained and needs to be understood by anyone with financial problems. An individual or business is insolvent when they cannot meet their financial commitments on the dates they become due.

This definition would of course classify most of us at some time or another as insolvent. Fail to pay that electricity bill on time and that person is technically insolvent. Most people know that it does not take very long for the debt collection system to gear up in the form of a red reminder notice.

Insolvency is not related to any kind of asset to debt ratios – unless assets can be sold quickly in order to release money to pay debts by their due date. People with assets worth far more than any debts that they had accumulated have been bankrupted simply because they were unable to meet their debt repayments on the date due. The odd missed or late payment is not a problem if the debtor is able to 'catch up' with their payments and bring themselves back into solvency i.e. are then able to meet their debt payments by their due date.

An individual or business has a problem when, for whatever reasons, they miss a payment/s and are unable to 'catch up'. What then tends to happen is that interest and charges will be applied to their account. If they again are unable to pay debts by their next due date then the situation will begin to spiral out of control. If there are several debts or one large debt then the interest and charges will, over a short period of time, be substantial.

Once insolvency has been recognised the next step is to assess the financial position. It is important that this step be carried out honestly and realistically as the information gathered will be used to determine which course of action to take.

Key concepts

The key concepts then, are that an individual is insolvent when they cannot meet their financial commitments when they fall due, and they become solvent again when they can, by whatever method, meet their financial commitments on time. This is the only sensible financial barometer that matters from the point of view of an individual debtor or business in trouble.

The aim for any particular insolvent individual or business is therefore very clearly defined i.e. to be in a position where they can meet their debt payments as and when they fall due – to become solvent again.

For any particular individual the methods of reaching their goal can be infinitely varied. Sometimes there will be a quick and easy solution – such as selling a high priced home, moving down market and clearing off a chain of debts at a stroke.

On other occasions a lot of negotiations will have to take place. This is because some individuals or businesses will have no easy options other than to enter into negotiations with many creditors.

The last resort for any debtor will be to wipe the slate clean and start again i.e. when all else fails he will be left with little option but to enter into bankruptcy.

Although there are a variety of methods to become solvent again any individual or business in debt is faced with four basic options. These are:

1) **Run away**

2) **Repay debts in full**

3) **Repay debts in part – in full and final settlement**

4) **Go bankrupt**

Step 1 is simply a silly option that we will discuss in the next chapter. The ultimate sanction that any debtor can face is bankruptcy. Each of the steps 2-3 are all realistic attempts to either avoid or prevent bankruptcy. Step 4 is the final solution if Steps 2-3 fail. It is important to have at least some knowledge of the subject of bankruptcy and to bear this in mind before attempting steps 2-3. The consequences of bankruptcy are described in Chapter 9 of this book.

3

Running Away

Some people simply decide to ignore their debt problems by not responding to any approaches or action from creditors or by simply running away from them. This may be done by moving house and leaving no forwarding address or even by fleeing abroad. This is not a realistic course of action and is not to be recommended at any time and under any circumstances.

The person who runs away is often constantly worrying about being caught up with (and at some stage creditors usually catch up) and has to live life in a constant state of trepidation. There are of course a few thick–skinned individuals who can perhaps live with such behaviour. These people are foolish for another, very important reason.

A person who runs away from his creditors by either ignoring them or fleeing the country can be bankrupted in his absence and for relatively small amounts. Any creditor owed £750 or more can apply to have a debtor bankrupted. If someone who runs away is bankrupted then that person will be held in bankruptcy until such time as he reappears. This means that if the person who ran away subsequently rebuilds his life and perhaps buys property he will lose all this if he is discovered later. We have known many people to whom this has happened.

For a person to adopt this course of action means that he must spend the rest of his life with a 'Sword of Damocles' hanging over his head. If a person is under such financial pressure that running away seems to be an attractive and realistic option, then it makes much more sense to at least go bankrupt first. This is because he will then at least be discharged from the bankruptcy after a few years and be able to breath easily again. So it simply makes no sense to run away. It is not only a silly action, it can turn out to be the hardest option of the avenues available.

4

The World of Debt Advice

In our view, it is always the best course of action for individuals to deal directly with creditors themselves. This is why we have produced this book. There are however, various outside sources of help, some of them useful, some of them dangerous. These are as follows:

Individual voluntary arrangements

It is possible for an individual to enter into a formal individual voluntary arrangement known as an IVA. These arrangements are legal contracts for the satisfaction of debt, either in whole or in part, and such arrangements, if voted in, are binding on all unsecured creditors, subject to limited technical exceptions that may cause difficulties.

The Bankruptcy Association was very keen on these arrangements when the first became available in 1987 and encouraged people to take this route. Bitter experience of seeing them fail time after time means we virtually never recommend this course of action. They are really just a pre-bankruptcy scam in very many cases. People are seduced into them because of an irrational fear of the alternatives. In addition, they often do not realise that in many cases when they have signed up to an IVA they have guaranteed that bankruptcy will follow. This is because many IVAs contain a clause that says that the supervisor of an IVA must apply for bankruptcy if an IVA subject fails to keep to the agreed terms.

The main reasons IVAs fail are that creditors often make excessive demands. In addition, inadequate or incorrect advice is given by so called professional advisers. These advisers can be insolvency practitioners or solicitors and others who gain substantial fees by enticing people into IVAs.

To sum up, even with the best intentions in the world, money tends to corrupt and, sadly, this procedure has proved just another example of that plain fact. IVAs are a 'financial product' proven by the fact that a multi-million pound industry has grown around them, proven by the fact that firms actively 'ambulance chase' debtors in order to 'sell' them an IVA, proven by the fact that IVAs are consistently failing, proven by the fact that the many people who enter into IVAs end up paying thousands of pounds to insolvency practitioners and are then bankrupted anyway, proven by the hundreds of complaints the Bankruptcy Association receives each year about failed IVAs. We say more about IVAs in the next chapter

Debt management companies

It is equally as important to be wary of the myriad of so called debt management companies and other debt advisers who advertise widely in local and national newspapers. These companies charge fees to manage a person's debts. Many are incompetent and inefficient. Many of their practices have been regularly exposed on various media and consumer programmes. Their charges are often excessive. Many of these firms are again just operating another scam taking advantage of the fear that many people in debt feel.

There is nothing these companies can do for a debtor that he cannot do better himself. Indeed, many creditors do not like dealing with these companies because they are losing out themselves because of the high charges they make. This reduces the amount available to creditors.

Other professional advice

Some debtors go to their solicitors or accountants to seek help with their debt problems. Neither of these professions are trained to advise on debt problems. Some solicitors do not even have the faintest knowledge of bankruptcy and insolvency matters as they mainly just have a general training in contract and family law. Accountants, of course, are trained to audit books.

In general (there are notable exceptions) people in these professions are no better placed to advise on debt problems than the average man in the street.

Citizen advice bureaux and other advice agencies

Most towns and cities have a variety of money advice sources ranging from Citizens Advice Bureaux to specialist money advice centres. The quality of these services varies enormously. Some CABs have experienced counsellors, other just work with volunteers who have limited knowledge and experience. There are national agencies as well such as ourselves – the Bankruptcy Association – and the National Debtline Service provided by the Birmingham Settlement.

The Bankruptcy Association is a totally independent organisation, supported by its members. It offers truly independent advice. The other organisations referred to above are often funded by a combination of taxpayers' money and donations from the larger moneylenders, such as banks.

Administration orders

Administration orders can be made by a county court against anyone who has a court order brought against them by their creditors. An administration order is an order made by a county court where an individual has to pay an agreed monthly amount to the court. This money is then distributed by the court to the individual's creditors. Administration orders are generally not an effective method of dealing with serious debt problems for a variety of reasons – not least local variations in the rules from one court to another. In our view, it is usually simpler and more effective for an individual in debt to deal with their creditors directly.

Commonsense and pragmatism is required

From the discussion above we hope it is clear to the reader that there are no miracle solutions to debt problems by seeking help elsewhere. The whole point of this book is to point out that any individual in debt who adopts a commonsense and pragmatic approach can often reach a solution with creditors to settle debts without the need for much, if any, outside help.

5

Outside Help
IVAs – Rescue or Rip-Off?

The Insolvency Act 1986 introduced what was, at the time, a new and apparently genuine way of dealing with overwhelming debt for businesses and individual debtors. It has become standard for insolvency practitioners to encourage individuals, partnerships and limited companies to enter such formal voluntary arrangements – known as IVAs for individuals and CVAs for companies.

How voluntary arrangements work

A voluntary arrangement is an offer put to creditors by an individual, business partners or limited companies to either sell off assets and/or, usually and, make a contribution from future earnings or profits to pay out a dividend to unsecured creditors in full settlement of their debts. The contract once accepted by a majority of unsecured creditors is legally binding on all other unsecured creditors.

Huge fees

Insolvency practitioners are very highly paid and they expect equally large fees, often several thousands of pounds up front – to begin with – and usually before an arrangement has even been voted on. If the arrangement is successful they continue to cream off further huge fees for the costs of administration. Indeed, with some if not most arrangements there is little or nothing left for the creditors after the insolvency practitioner has taken his substantial cut.

Successful at first

Naïve as I was in 1987 when these arrangements were first introduced, I thought they were a brilliant concept. Indeed, I thought they might bring bankruptcy proceedings virtually to an end. Within a year of the new legislation being in place the insolvency profession, particularly the larger firms, backed by their client banks, had effectively sabotaged the new procedures. They simply demanded – and continue to do so – much more from debtors than they could realistically afford to pay. It also became standard procedure to lock debtors into making payments over a five-year period – whereas payments in bankruptcy are only made for three years, until discharge occurs.

Soon these voluntary arrangements were failing in droves and people were subsequently forced into bankruptcy, after having to struggle – sometimes for years – to make substantial payments into the agreement, most of which was – and still is – used to cover insolvency practitioner's fees. Since their introduction in 1987 I have rarely seen a single situation where I have felt that a voluntary arrangement was an appropriate course of action for any person or company in debt. If a deal can be struck with creditors, it can be done more effectively informally, without the costs that formal procedures involve.

Clauses that guarantee bankruptcy

Furthermore many voluntary arrangements contain clauses that require the terms of the arrangement to be strictly adhered to. The law is such that if a debtor is even a few hours late in making stage payment the arrangement is deemed by the court to have failed. The Bankruptcy Association has had many cases where people have been paying into a voluntary arrangement religiously for several years, have missed a payment and then have been bankrupted anyway. The bankruptcy then lasts for a further three years where anything they have left is taken from them.

Failure rates kept well hidden

We have tried to obtain the true failure rates for these arrangements for several years but because of the nature of the Insolvency Service and the way the statistics are kept we are unable to access the true figure. The figure is extremely high because we speak to hundreds of people each year struggling to cope with voluntary arrangements.

It is neither in the interest of the Government's Insolvency Service – who have plans to join in this scam – nor of the insolvency profession to reveal the true extent of the failure rate for voluntary arrangements. Voluntary arrangements have quickly developed into a multi-million pound rip-off industry. Those who are making money from them wish to continue to do so – the Government included.

Usually, debtors signing up for voluntary arrangements are signing up for extended penury and a guaranteed bankruptcy when it is just that situation that they are trying to avoid. Threatened bankruptcy and irrational fear of the system based on ignorance are extremely powerful incitements used to push honest, decent people – who turn to others for help – into an IVA agreement and an extended bankruptcy. Having directly asked the Prime Minister and the head of the Insolvency Service for comment on these matters they continue stubbornly not to do so – their silence speaks volumes.

Informal arrangements are often the best answer

The sadness of the above is compounded by the fact that it can be relatively simple, for little or no cost at all, for individuals and companies to make their own informal arrangements with their creditors. The only advantage a formal voluntary arrangement has over an informal one is that a 75 per cent majority of creditors is needed to vote an IVA in, compared to getting all the creditors to agree to a self negotiated one.

In reality, because of the flexibility of an informal arrangement (and with no built in bankruptcy trigger) the debtor is often able to convince all creditors into agreeing to a deal. Once a number of creditors have agreed to a deal it is easier to convince those who have not initially agreed, to fall into line.

In any event, because the expensive fees to enter into a formal voluntary arrangement have been saved, some of this money can be used to pay off small awkward creditors – it is often the creditor owed the least who is the most awkward. A further point is that some creditors deliberately vote against formal voluntary arrangements because they take exception to so much of the money on offer being taken by an insolvency practitioner. Creditors are well aware where the money creamed off goes to in a formal arrangement. They also know that they have a better chance of seeing a substantial return through an informal arrangement.

Irrational fear

What leads so many people to try for a formal voluntary arrangement? It is because they have an irrational fear of bankruptcy. They do not seem to realise that surviving a formal bankruptcy can be easier than struggling with a formal voluntary arrangement with all its inherent disadvantages. They are encouraged in these irrational fears by the sharks of the Government led insolvency world who circle them looking for plunder.

6

Ground Rules

Before showing how to conduct debt negotiations with creditors it is important for the reader to fully understand the basic ground rules used to deal with debt problems. The starting point for anyone or any business in financial difficulty is to carefully and honestly examine their weekly or monthly budget.

Although this sounds like an elementary exercise the vast majority of people in debt simply have little idea of their true income and expenditure. Having a written budget is one of the most fundamental concepts in dealing with debt. In fact, once a budget has been drawn up in black and white many people can see where the answer to their financial problems lies.

Budgeting

By definition it will follow that the budgets (although they may not formally exist) of the majority of insolvent individuals are out of balance. Therefore the obvious starting point for anyone struggling to cope with debt is to draw up a simple weekly or monthly budget. This does not need to be a complicated affair – in fact a simple budget makes it much easier to understand what is happening to a person's finances.

It is important on this point for people to be totally honest with themselves and to include all income and expenditure. No matter how insignificant an expenditure may seem it should be included. Both ordinary consumer debtors the self-employed in business need to carry out this important exercise. In the case of self-employed people they should state an 'estimated' income and indicate that this is the case.

Example monthly budget for Mr A Thomas

Monthly Income	£	Monthly Expenditure	£
Your wage	1,400	Mortgage	350
Partners wage		Endowment policy	50
Unemployment benefit		2nd Mortgage	100
Pension		Rent	
Family Credit		Council Tax	50
Income support		Telephone	20
Housing benefit		Water	10
Single parent benefit		Gas	20
Invalidity benefit		Electricity	40
Maintenance		Home Insurance	20
Other income		Life insurance	25
		Car insurance	15
		Car tax	10
		Maintenance	30
		Child care	
		TV Rental/License/satellite	60
		Housekeeping	250
TOTAL	1,400	TOTAL	1050

OTHER CREDITORS		
Name of company	Total outstanding £	Monthly payment £
TKE Bank	10,000	250
GRB Card	5,000	140
TOTAL	15,000	390

In this example, Mr Thomas has a budget that is out of balance by £40 each month. As Mr Thomas cannot meet all of his financial commitments from his budget he needs to consider the following:

Increase income (perhaps through overtime or a part-time job, or by checking that all appropriate government allowances are being claimed – such as child tax credits).

Reduce all unnecessary expenditure (is satellite television or that rented video recorder really necessary?)

Assistance from friends and family

Some people may be fortunate enough to have friends and relatives willing to help them to solve their debt problems. A gift or interest free loan may provide a solution to debt problems. We cannot stress enough the need for caution should this avenue be considered.

It can be the case that funds from friend and family sources only partially solve debt problems and people have ended up bankrupt anyway. In these cases the funds provided by the relatives have simply been wasted.

It is important for anyone borrowing funds or indeed accepting a gift of money to supposedly help them, that they view their current problems realistically. Many people fail to face up to the magnitude of their financial position and live in the hope that they are able to put the matter right. This can be the case even where there is little realistic possibility of doing so. It is very distressing trying to cope with debts, but it is even worse if funds from friends and family are also lost in a failed attempt to resolve the problem. This should always be borne in mind by anyone seeking financial assistance from friends or relatives. Only accept such help if it will indeed solve the problem and not just buy a little more time. Otherwise this is just wasting an important back up resource.

Refinancing

Although the old adage 'never borrow from Peter to pay Paul' may have made sense in the context of our grandparents' way of life, it is definitely not true today in a social context of widespread property ownership.

Very often it makes sense to replace one type of debt with another. For example, it makes perfect sense to replace a string of credit card debts on high rates of interest with a secured second mortgage on a much lower rate of interest and therefore a smaller monthly repayment. People in debt however, need to be aware that there are rogue loan sharks about who offer second mortgages at crippling rates of interest and who also charge fees for arranging that second mortgage. Therefore when seeking or considering a second mortgage several quotes should be sought and any arrangement fees should be seriously queried as a matter of course.

Consolidation loans can also help, but it is important to be aware that the person on the telephone is also a sales person. Their job is to sell debt. What tends to happen is that they will consolidate existing debts into one loan, extend the period over which payments are to be made – hence lower monthly payments and they often offer extra money. This does not always solve the debt problem. Sometimes it merely adds to it. Consolidation loans may help, but again they should be approached with caution.

If the problem cannot be resolved by any of these methods then more drastic action needs to be considered. This first action is to prioritise debts and ensure that they are paid in priority order.

Priority Debts

Certain debts are known to money advisers as priority debts. Thus any debts that may lead to imprisonment, such as court fines, council tax and maintenance orders have a high priority and should be paid first.

Other high priority debts are those that may lead to the loss of the home. These may be mortgage payments or rent payments.

Further priority debts are the major utilities i.e. gas, electricity and water. Failure to pay utility bills will lead to these supplies eventually being cut off.

The next priority debts are any hire purchase debts. If these payments are not maintained, then the lender may be able to quickly seize these goods. Some people may have some slightly different priority debts. A student for example, may need to pay a course fee to further their education. In such a case the course fee would be a priority debt. It is simple common sense to give these particular debts priority.

It is however, amazing how many people pay off less important debts first. This is usually due to the methods employed by non-priority creditors. For example, they will use telephone calls or threatening letters to pressure a debtor into making payment. It is important to note that an unsecured creditor, such as a credit card company, cannot harm a debtor in the short term in the way that a gas or electricity company can by cutting off fuel supplies.

Debts such as unsecured credit cards, store cards etc should be paid last and then only when there is enough money left to do so.

Self-employed people have an additional set of priority debts that follow after the above have been dealt with. These are statutory debts to the tax authorities and also business rates. The tax authorities nearly always demand that their debts be paid in full or they will eventually move to bankrupt those who fail to pay them. Similarly, local authorities are very aggressive about unpaid business rates. For the self-employed to avoid bankruptcy it is important that they keep clear of these debts because the rules of negotiations that apply to most creditors do not apply to these statutory bodies. They are much more difficult to deal with.

Secured creditors

Secured creditors are creditors who have their debt secured against the property or assets of debtors. Mortgage debts are invariably secured against the property of the borrower. Other creditors, such as banks, often ask for second or third charges on someone's property when advancing a business loan for example.

Secured creditors are therefore in a different league to other creditors. They may have the right to repossess someone's home or property if they do not make the agreed repayments. These creditors must therefore always be paid first as there is virtually no defence mechanism that can be deployed against them.

Dealing with angry creditors

The usual line that creditors take when people default on their debts is that 'you borrowed the money and you should pay it back.' Sometimes the sense of anger is very real. A small builder who is not paid for work by a customer might well feel genuine fury and upset. Other creditors such as credit card companies and finance companies employ professional and well practiced techniques such as using stern letters and aggressive telephone calls to give voice to this anger. So debtors are generally faced with a wall of stern indignation and intimidation. This problem needs to be dealt with in a professional manner.

Telephone calls from creditors

Many creditors use the telephone as an aggressive form of psychological intimidation, ringing people at all times of the day and night and often being quite insulting. The telephone has little or no place to play in debt negotiations and should be removed from the scene of action quickly. When negotiating with creditors a calm air is required. This cannot be achieved when a debtor has to cope with this type of pressure.

Only deal with creditors by letter. Creditors should be made aware, in writing, that telephone calls from them will not be tolerated. If creditors ring, on any matter, then the debtor should simply state that:

'I am sorry but I do not discuss my private financial affairs over the telephone with anyone – goodbye'

He should then put the telephone down immediately after saying goodbye. The creditor's agent will only keep on with his diatribe unless the debtor ends the conversation. Anyone in debt will receive these types of telephone calls – it is part of the debt collection system. The creditor's agent will think nothing of it and simply move onto the next number their computer throws up. Never fall into the trap of feeling that this is in anyway unacceptable – that is how they keep you talking and how they cause upset and in many cases how they get people to pay. Anyone in debt should instinctively say the above phase as soon as they realise that they are talking to a creditors agent.

There is no need to worry about the technicalities about what is or is not legal harassment. It simply requires a point blank refusal to discuss personal financial affairs on the telephone and is a perfectly reasonable and legal position to adopt. This will quickly end the problem if applied, as a matter of course, with every telephone call from creditors. The other simple solutions are to change the telephone number and go ex-directory or even cut the telephone off. Do not put up with telephone pressure.

Letters and default notices from creditors

People who default on their debt instalments also tend to get bombarded with a variety of formal looking demand notices and official default notices. This is all part of the psychological warfare that creditors deploy against debtors. Always reply to letters from creditors and always by writing. If there are many creditors it is simplest to set aside one day each month when all correspondence is replied to.

Debt collection agencies and solicitors

Many creditors pass over the chase for their money to a variety of debt collection agencies and sometimes to firms of solicitors. These people should be dealt with in exactly the same way as when dealing directly with a creditor. Again they are part of the psychological pressure that creditors deploy. The fact that they are solicitors or a debt collection agency makes no difference to the debtor's position or attitude towards them.

Court orders

It is very expensive these days for a creditor to issue a court summons for a debt to try to force payment with the legal weight of a court behind it. They are unlikely to take this course of action against someone who is regularly writing to them. It is when people completely ignore creditors that they go to the expense and trouble of obtaining a court order.

Court summonses must also be dealt with immediately. Fill any reply forms in immediately making an offer of a regular payment. It is also in order to add in a letter when replying to a court summons explaining the general financial position in respect of other creditors.

Creditors can cause debtors a fair amount of hassle and discomfort if they are willing to spend more of their money deploying the full panoply of power of the courts. People can be questioned about their income by the court, wages can be restrained, and bailiffs can be deployed to seize goods from a debtor's home. Such actions will rarely be deployed by creditors against debtors who keep in regular communication with them.

Anyone who is unfortunate enough to find themselves involved with a lot of court problems or who are getting hassle from bailiffs calling on them would be wise to seek direct advice from the Bankruptcy Association as to how to tackle matters.

Such people may have to consider bankruptcy because bankruptcy brings an end to these sorts of problems. Details of how to take up membership of the Bankruptcy Association are in the back of this book.

Do not be an ostrich

In my experience advising over 20,000 people who have passed through the Bankruptcy Association the most serious problem that debtors face is their own failure to deal with pressing matters. Debt problems can bring with them blurred judgement and an inability to think straight. This problem affects everyone in debt to some degree or other. It is not pleasant to face up to financial problems. However, it must be done, even if the help of a third party, such as a friend or relative, is sought to achieve this.

We cannot stress enough how it is often inactivity on the part of debtors that so often brings about the worst possible outcomes to debt problems. The sad truth is that some people simply cannot be helped because of their psychological inability to deal with the worry pressure. On the other hand, some people – once the simplicity of negotiating with creditors is pointed out to them – positively thrive on getting to grips with their problems. One member of the Bankruptcy Association after being given the advice offered in this book promptly came to sensible arrangements with all his sixty-eight creditors, a remarkable achievement.

Take control

The point of all the above is to show how the debtor, as far as is possible, is able to take control of what might appear to be an out of control dilemma. By firmly adhering to the above rules, in most cases a high degree of calmness will be achieved. Remember also that the advice offered in this book is based on a tried and tested formula that has worked out in reality many, many times. It is all about 'taking control' and driving everyone along to the correct and sensible solution.

The best analogy is with that of a defeated army that has just lost a major battle. If the army turns into a fleeing rabble the advancing enemy will slaughter the retreating soldiers. But if they retreat in good order, fighting rearguard actions to slow the enemy advance and destroying bridges and supplies along the way, then they will almost certainly live to fight another day. Such an army, although it has lost a battle, still has some control over its future destiny.

Deploy a repetitive standard procedure to deal with creditors

Creditors usually deploy repetitive standard procedures to harass debtors. Therefore the real secret when dealing with creditors is to organise a repetitive standard procedure of replying to them. Hit them with their own tactics. In fact, this is essentially what creditors are looking for. For creditors, debtors are unofficially grouped into two categories – 'those who can't pay and those who won't pay'. Essentially a debtor who does not keep in communication with his creditors 'won't pay' and those who do 'can't pay'. Therefore anyone responding in a clear, consistent, regular, systemised fashion will satisfy creditors that they 'can't pay' but are 'trying to pay'. The best way to do this is to:

1) Always write to creditors each month explaining that the due payment cannot be made.

2) Always enclose a nominal payment with the letter e.g. £5 or an amount that can be sensibly afforded (nothing irritates creditors more than promises of payment, because most people fail to keep to their promises). Sending even a small amount of money on a regular basis enhances the credibility of a debtor enormously.

3) Direct creditors to the 'final solution' to the problem with them e.g. that they will have to agree to new terms or bankruptcy may ensue to no-ones benefit.

7

Repay Debts in Full

Depending on the size of the debts involved and the circumstances of particular individuals it may be possible, through a restructuring of finances, to cope with the debt position and repay the debts in full.

In such a circumstance all that a person requires from creditors is the time to pay. It is important to negotiate for this time however. We pointed out earlier that a person can be bankrupted who has assets and property worth more than the debts he owes. It is surprising how many people fail to realise this. Courts may, and do, make bankruptcy orders against people who owe £750 or more, regardless of the value of their assets.

Negotiating with Creditors

Sensible negotiations with creditors are very often the best possible way of dealing with such short-term cash flow problems. The majority of creditors (although by no means all) are reasonable people and will adopt a more sympathetic line if they are made aware of the problem and offered some sensible proposals.

They will very often, if personal circumstances merit it, be prepared to extend the period that was originally agreed for repayment. If a proper explanation is provided and details of income and expenditure are made available, then most creditors will be accommodating about allowing extra time to pay and may even suspend any further interest charges.

The negotiation is a simple game of mathematics. Always remember this. It is important to keep emotions and personal feelings towards the creditors out of any negotiation.

Constructing an offer for creditors

The aim of this negotiation is to request for an extended period of time for payment of a debt or debts and to put a stop on interest and charges being applied to the account. This is for people in debt who could manage to continue to make debt payments once they have 'caught up'. Again, it is important to be realistic. People in debt who have no prospect of being able to fulfil future debt payments should read the next chapter.

Basically someone who believes he can repay his debts in full if he is allowed some extra time to do so should not face too many problems. Such a person is behaving perfectly reasonably from the creditors point of view.

Creditors like to have their debts paid in full if possible, as we all do. Someone who is seeking to repay his debts in full is really a superior kind of debtor and should expect some realistic help from creditors.

The first step is to construct a statement of financial affairs.

Monthly Income		£	Monthly Expenditure		£
Your wage		1,400	Mortgage		350
Partners wage			Endowment policy		50
Unemployment benefit			2nd Mortgage		100
Pension			Rent		0
Family Credit			Council Tax		50
Income support			Telephone		20
Housing benefit			Water		10
Single parent benefit			Gas		20
Invalidity benefit			Electricity		40
Maintenance			Home Insurance		20
Other income (specify)			Life insurance		25
			Car insurance		15
			Car tax		10
			Maintenance		30
			Child care		0
			TV Rental/License		60
			Housekeeping		250
TOTAL	£	1,400	TOTAL	£	1050

OTHER CREDITORS		
Name of company	Total outstanding	Monthly payment currently required
TKE Bank	10,000	200
GRB Card	5,000	100
BG Company	10,000	200
TOTAL £	25,000	500

I declare that this is an accurate record of my financial position as at:

Date: *1 April*   **Signed:** *Mr A Thomas*

27

The second step is to construct a covering letter outlining the position. For Mr Thomas the solution is to offer to each creditor £50 less than his normal payment. The letter that follows is a template letter asking for extended payment terms from TKE Bank to whom he should normally be paying £200 each month. He would also reduce payments to his other creditors by the same amount (using the same template letter) and ask for a hold to be put on interest and charges.

1 April

Mr J Abraham *(Name and address of creditor)*
TKE Bank
Halton Buildings
46 Halton Lane
Lancaster
LA4 6BR

Dear Mr Abraham,

Re: Mr A Thomas, 12 The Mews, Eastham, Essex. (Name and address of debtor)

Account: 00123456   (Account number/reference details)

I enclose a statement of my financial affairs. My financial circumstances have changed because I was recently made redundant and I am now in a much lower paid job.

As you can see from my statement of financial affairs I am unable to meet my current debt repayments as they fall due. I would therefore ask if you could extend my payment period in order to reduce monthly payments to a level that I can realistically manage to meet. The amount I can afford to pay you each month is £150 (enter amount that can be afforded) and I enclose a cheque for this amount.

I would also ask in view of my financial situation, if you would put a stop on charges and interest being applied to my account as these will continue to prevent me from meeting my debt obligations.

If you were to do this I would, as can be seen from my statement of financial affairs, be able to meet these reduced payments and repay my debt in full in due course.

I would be grateful for your earliest reply.

Yours sincerely

Mr A Thomas

Under no circumstances ask for permission to send a lower payment – just send it. Never write to a creditor promising payment. As mentioned earlier, creditors know from experience that promises of payment are rarely fulfilled and doing this only serves to antagonise creditors and weakens a debtor's position.

If necessary the same letter and statement of financial affairs should be sent to any other creditors. Should a creditor be unsympathetic and refuse then it is important to try again and keep trying. The same letter should be sent every month with a statement of financial affairs, until they accept. It is important to ensure that a payment is sent with each monthly letter.

Usually creditors will expect evidence of earnings and expenditure. If creditors ask for this information then it should be supplied. By being co-operative and adopting a sensible attitude towards creditors, people should be able to resolve temporary debt problems.

Most creditors adopt a sensible attitude towards people who owe them money. They will want to see the debt repayments continue. It is not in their interest to bankrupt someone for the simple reason that they will see little or no financial return if they do so. In many cases, provided the necessary information has been given and a commitment to future payments has been shown, they will accept such offers and thus the debtor is able to return to solvency. If they do not then the debtor has no alternative but to take the more drastic action outlined in the following chapters.

8

Repay Debts in Part – in Full and Final Settlement

I will begin by explaining what the title of this chapter means. It simply means that if someone owes a creditor say £10,000, it is possible to ask that creditor to accept £1,000 in full and final settlement of that debt. If the creditor accepts such an offer it means that the creditor has agreed to forgive £9,000 – the balance of the debt. Once such a deal has been agreed in writing and the £1,000 paid over to the creditor then the debtor is then freed of the entire debt. Thousands of such deals are done each year in the United Kingdom.

It is rarely possible for someone with assets greater than their debts to strike such deals. Someone who owns a home outright worth £100,000 for example and who owes creditors £50,000 would be expected to sell that home to repay his debts in full. Creditors will not forgive debts to people they believe can pay in full. The same also applies to people on high incomes with plenty of disposable income after living expenses have been met. This is plain commonsense – but needs to be stated here.

For people in business, it is generally impossible to do deals for partial repayments of debt owed to tax authorities and for business or domestic rates. These statutory bodies will always demand repayment in full.

The tactics described in this chapter however can be applied to most other debts, including bank and finance company debts, trade creditors, credit card debts or mortgage shortfalls. The rules of the negotiating game are the same for a business debtor as they are for a consumer debtor. There is only the one method.

We have dealt with people in serious debt for decades. We have also helped hundreds of people to avoid bankruptcy by the application of the methods described in this book. The system does not guarantee success (sometimes just one awkward creditor can force a bankruptcy), but it does offer the best opportunity of a successful outcome. And if a successful outcome is not achieved by applying this advice at least the reader will have a sort of satisfaction in knowing that all rational methods to achieve a happy outcome have been tried.

The secret for success is to initially make an offer that can be easily met, leaving leeway to increase any offer by increments if the first offer is refused as it usually will be. The other important point to note is that there is no end point for these negotiations until and if bankruptcy is forced. Sometimes negotiations may last over many months or even years.

The terms 'creditors' and 'debtors' are words that cover a huge multiplicity of real life characters. Creditors can range from cool-headed professional negotiators from financial institutions to a furious builder howling for blood over an unpaid bill. Debtors include people with a strong moral desire to repay all their debts in full, down to people who feel that repaying 1 pence in the pound is asking too much from them.

Importance of credibility

Readers should therefore understand that before they start negotiations they must establish a degree of credibility with creditors. Creditors need to feel they are negotiating with someone who understands their side of the case. They will quickly recognize amateurish behaviour displayed by the negotiating debtor. Such a person will be quickly discredited and creditors will refuse to deal with him.

It is also important when negotiating to tell the truth (within reason). Anyone who tries to weave a general web of deceit will generally be uncovered and the consequence will be a total loss of credibility with creditors, bringing an end to any chance of a successful outcome. However, stretching or bending the truth a little is not unreasonable. After all, this is a matter of the financial life or death of the debtor. He needs to have a life worth living at the end of the day.

Making an offer of part payment – in full and final settlement

Creditors normally expect to be repaid in full. That is the basis on which money is lent and money is borrowed. If, however, it is made clear to creditors that if they do not agree to accept a proportion of their debt in full and final settlement the only alternative will be for the borrower to enter into bankruptcy, thereby giving them a nil return on their debt, then most creditors will give such an offer serious consideration provided they believe that this is the true position of the debtor. This often takes time and patience but persistence often pays off. Taking the route of bankruptcy can prove to be just as longwinded and painful. Therefore the easier route should at least be tried first.

The Bankruptcy Association once did a negotiation for a young man with a very aggressive creditor, a finance company. We had offered the company £1,000 eventually as a final offer to settle a debt of £12,000. This was flatly refused. We therefore advised the young man to go into bankruptcy as the only way left of dealing with the debt. Fortunately he did not follow our advice and he simply did nothing.

Six months after the end of the negotiations we received a phone call from the finance company. It was from the new credit manager for the company and she told me she could not understand why our offer had not been accepted. She would be happy to settle on those terms. So the young man paid up and bankruptcy was avoided.

This incident has taught us that you never give up on these matters. Sometimes, the simple passage of time brings a solution. There is always a solution to debt problems, even if it ultimately means bankruptcy.

If a creditor is to accept a proportion of the debt in full and final settlement, then that creditor will usually expect the agreed amount to be paid by way of a lump sum payment. For example, a creditor may agree to accept a single payment of £500 to settle a £2,000 debt. They would be extremely unlikely to accept an offer of £50 a month paid over ten months. Creditors know from long experience that instalment deals more often than not break down and do not last the course. In addition, they have the administration costs to bear of these slow repayments. It is always better therefore to offer a single lump sum repayment.

The initial offer made to creditors will not be the real limit of the offer that a debtor might be finally prepared to make. This is where the boundaries between truth and untruth become blurred. It is common sense for a debtor to be cagey in his initial offer, as he needs leeway to increase the offer.

Creditors themselves will also take the opportunity to be cagey in their responses. It is a well-known truism that no human being is ever a hundred per cent truthful about their financial affairs. Even husbands and wives hold back financial information from each other.

It is quite natural that a debtor, for example, will hold back the fact that she sports a pair of diamond earrings given to her as a keepsake by her grandmother and worth £2,000. Real life never produces clean, neat solutions to problems. This is particularly true when negotiating over money.

Sometimes too, negotiations may prove successful say with 5 creditors owed a total of £10,000 who agree to accept 10p in the pound, but there is one awkward creditor owed a mere £750 who refuses to agree. It is often the case that the smallest creditors are the hardest to crack. In such a case, if the money can be raised to pay that awkward creditor in full and sweep them out of the way, this would make perfect sense.

We pointed out earlier that it important to understand when trying to negotiate along the above lines that creditors will have to be satisfied that the debtor is willing to give up any available assets. For example, if someone owed £50,000 and that person owned a home with £30,000 of equity available if it were to be sold, then the creditor would expect at least this amount of money to be made available to them.

Creditors will only be prepared to accept a proportion of the debt in full and final settlement if the debtor has no disposable income and/or very few assets. The creditor will require evidence to prove this. A debtor cannot expect a creditor to accept a loss and leave him, the debtor with assets and/or disposable income. However, a debtor who owns a property which has very little equity in it, say just a few thousand pounds, should expect to be treated as though he has no equity. This is because, if that person were to be bankrupted, then the costs of the bankruptcy would leave nothing over for creditors when a property was sold in such a circumstance.

This solution to debt problems is often a long term one. It is no quick fix. A debtor will have to be tough and patient. In addition, it may not work and, as previously mentioned, a creditor may determinedly refuse any offers in which case the debtor is really given no alternative but to consider bankruptcy.

The basic plan on the following pages may be adapted for any debtor with any number of creditors. It does not matter if that person is an ordinary consumer debtor with some credit cards debts he cannot repay or if it is a businessman with a score of trade creditors chasing him. The basic steps are the same for anyone who is going to try and do a deal for part-repayment in full and final settlement. These are:

Step 1: Make it clear to creditors that it is no longer possible to repay the debt. It must be made crystal clear to creditors that any debt owed to them has been well and truly defaulted on and that the debtor is genuinely unable to pay. A creditor will not do a deal with someone who is up to date with his current repayments on a credit card or who has just paid his last month's trade debts.

Step 2: On a monthly basis, always write a letter apologising for this, explaining the position and always enclosing a nominal payment, say £5 (or an amount that can be sensibly afforded).

Step 3: After defaulting on debts for at least 12 months and preferably for longer (we said it was a long haul), the process can begin of making offers for part payment – in full and final settlement of the debts.

Remember such tactics are of no use with secured creditors, court fines, maintenance, tax debts and rates debts. These types of debts are generally non-negotiable and must be paid in full.

In the example case we will use a fictitious person - Mr Thomas, who is in serious debt difficulties

There are two simple steps to take when starting to negotiate with creditors.

Step 1 – Constructing a statement of financial affairs.

Step 2 – Constructing a covering letter.

Step 1: Construct a statement of financial affairs

Monthly Income	£	Monthly Expenditure	£
Your wage	1,400	Mortgage	350
Partners wage		Endowment policy	50
Unemployment benefit		2nd Mortgage	300
Pension		Rent	
Family Credit		Council Tax	50
Income support		Telephone	20
Housing benefit		Water	10
Single parent benefit		Gas	20
Invalidity benefit		Electricity	40
Other income (Specify)		Home Insurance	20
		Life insurance	25
		Car insurance	15
		Car tax	10
		Maintenance	130
		TV Rental/License	10
		Housekeeping	315
TOTAL £	1,400	TOTAL £	1,365

OTHER CREDITORS		
Name of company	Total outstanding £	Monthly payment offer £
TKE Bank	10, 000	5
GRB Card	5, 000	5
BG Company	15, 000	5
SM Bank	5, 000	5
BG Bank	20, 000	5
AWD Card	2, 500	5
SHK Credit	15, 000	5
TOTAL	72, 500	35

I declare that this is an accurate record of my financial position as at:
Date: *1 April*   **Signed:** *Mr A Thomas*

Step 2: Construct a covering letter

---

1 April

Mr J Abraham *(Name and address of creditor)*
TKE Bank
Halton Buildings
46 Halton Lane
Lancaster
LA4 6BR

Dear Mr Abraham,

Re: Mr A Thomas, 12 The Mews, Eastham, Essex. (Name and address of debtor)

Account: 00123456   (Account number/reference details)

I enclose a statement of my financial affairs. As can be seen from my statement of financial affairs I am unable to meet my current debt repayments as they fall due. This is because (give full reasons here e.g. that my business has failed or I have been made redundant). I also have no assets or property that are available to creditors.

I ask in view of my financial situation, if you would stop charges and interest being applied to my account, as I am unable to meet this month's total debt repayment. I am however able to manage £5.00 in respect of the debt and I enclose a cheque for this amount.

I would also request that you do not take court action against me. Such an action on your part may force me into bankruptcy in which case no dividend would be payable to yourselves.

I will let you know if and when my circumstances change.

Yours sincerely

Mr A Thomas

The end game

By following the steps previously outlined it is unlikely that creditors will pursue expensive legal avenues to recover their money. Because they are receiving regular monthly communications and token payments, this makes the creditors aware that the debtor is genuinely trying to deal with their financial problems. It also makes creditors aware that they are unlikely to recover the full amount of the debt owed to them.

After at least a year of writing a monthly letter to creditors and making token payments, the debtor will be in a position to play the 'end game' by trying to negotiate a settlement of their debts by making an offer in full and final settlement. The amount of the offer will depend upon the funds available to the debtor, perhaps from a family member or friend.

There are no hard and fast rules for the amount that should be offered. The Bankruptcy Association once agreed a deal with a mortgage company to settle a shortfall debt of £68,000 for the sum of £500 in full and final settlement. This was for a single mother, in rented accommodation and studying at university.

In another case, for a married couple that were both working and earning good money, a similar mortgage shortfall was settled for the sum of £4,000. Negotiating with creditors is not an exact science. They are an art form that should be conducted with pragmatic commonsense.

The basic rule is to work out how much can be realistically raised by the debtor. In our example, Mr Thomas knows he can raise the necessary £14,500 as his son will loan him the money. He should start by offering half the amount his son can actually raise (£7,250), on a pro rata basis.

Pro rata

Pro rata simply means that the debtor offers all creditors a percentage in the pound. It is important to offer all the creditors the same percentage in the pound. Therefore a creditor owed £10,000 is offered 10 pence in the pound (£1,000) and a creditor owed £5,000 is also offered 10 pence in the pound (£500) and so on. In the sample letter that follows we provide and example of how this is done. Template offer letter to settle a debt

---

1 April

Mr J Abraham *(Name and address of creditor)*
TKE Bank
Halton Buildings
46 Halton Lane
Lancaster
LA4 6BR

Dear Mr Abraham,

Re: Mr A Thomas, 12 The Mews, Eastham, Essex. (Name and address of debtor)

Account: 00123456   (Account number/reference details)

I enclose a statement of my financial affairs and monthly payment of £5.00. It is clear that due to my current financial circumstances that I will never be able to repay in full my debt to you. As a result I may have to consider entering into bankruptcy if I am unable to reach a settlement with you.

My son is willing to raise a loan of £7,250 to reach a settlement with my creditors. In total I owe all of my creditors £72,500. I enclose my most recent financial statement showing these. I am therefore able offer a pro rata offer of 10 pence in the pound to all my creditors if they will accept this in full and final settlement of my debts.

My debt to you currently stands at £10,000. I am therefore prepared to offer you the sum of £1,000 payable to you within 30 days, if you will accept this payment in full and final settlement of my debt to you. I would be grateful for your earliest reply

Yours sincerely

Mr A Thomas

Some creditors may accept the first offer. If they do – pay them off. Other creditors may refuse. In these cases leeway has been allowed to raise the offer, as only half the amount really available has been offered. Another letter should be sent raising the offer from 10 pence in the pound to 12 pence in the pound, saying that this can only be done with difficulty.

Mr Thomas will be prepared to ultimately raise his offer to 20 pence in the pound, the top offer that can sensibly be raised. In many cases, creditors will eventually settle because they benefit by doing so. If they refuse his final offer Mr Thomas can either keep repeating it in the hope that his creditors will eventually accept, or he will have to consider going bankrupt.

Token payments

Whilst pro rata offers are made to try to ultimately settle debts in full and final payment it is not necessary to make pro rata token payments. Some agencies advise that this should be done. In practice it is simply too complicated to manage regular token payments by this method. It is simplest to send each creditor the same token payment which is really just acknowledging that the debt exists until a final deal can be struck.

Annual reviews

Creditors usually review their payment arrangements with debtors once each year. They will normally write asking debtors to ring them to discuss future payments. People in debt should understand that this is just another aspect of the debt collection system designed to harass and intimidate debtors into making higher payments.

The response to this tactic is to send the normal offer letter and statement of financial affairs with their normal token payment along with a covering letter stating that 'as can be seen from by statement of financial affairs my situation has not changed. I do not wish to deal with this matter by telephone. Thank you'. The secret to any negotiation is to never be intimidated by creditors.

9

Go Bankrupt

Bankruptcy is the ultimate sanction that can be brought against any debtor. It is also the ultimate sanction that a debtor can bring against his creditors! Many people have heard of bankruptcy and few people would relish the prospect of going bankrupt. Yet many people know little of the real effects of bankruptcy or the reasons for going bankrupt.

Bankruptcy is a dirty word in our society and implies that a person has done something illegal or at the least underhand. This is not the case. The majority of bankrupts are decent, honourable human beings who have, for many different reasons, succumbed to the pressures of debt.

When and why to go bankrupt

Bankruptcy is seen as a humiliating process and, indeed, it sometimes is. Some have to be dragged through the process kicking and screaming. Others are glad of the relief from pursuing creditors that a bankruptcy order brings. The first rule for people in financial difficulties is to set aside their own internalised feelings and look at their problems objectively.

Take the hypothetical case of Peter who has run a business that has failed. He has sold his home in an attempt to stave off business collapse, but in the end he has failed and is left with no assets. Peter is now in rented accommodation, unemployed and saddled with debts totalling tens of thousands of pounds all of which are causing him desperate worry.

In this example, Peter has in effect already suffered the worst effects of business failure and debt i.e. the loss of his home and occupation. He now stands to gain some relief from a bankruptcy. Although he may not relish the idea of bankruptcy it will at least protect him from the actions of aggressive creditors. He should only take this course of action, however, when he has exhausted all possibilities of reaching a settlement with creditors described in early chapters.

It is this kind of pragmatic reasoning that needs to be applied by people in financial difficulties. People in debt can be compared to the captain of a sinking ship. A prudent captain will do all that he can to prevent his ship from sinking. It would however, be foolish if the ship were to go down with all hands as a result of his efforts. At some point he must save his crew and himself and what possessions he can, by taking to the lifeboats. Bankruptcy may be, in some cases, the lifeboat that a person in debt must take to after considering the alternatives.

During the course of his bankruptcy, as long as he does not inherit or win money, or earn more than he needs to live to a reasonable standard, he will not be required to make any payments to his official receiver or trustee in bankruptcy. Upon discharge he will be free to rebuild his life anew, although this can be difficult because of the stigma that bankruptcy brings.

The previous chapters describe the methods of avoiding bankruptcy. In many cases, however, it simply cannot be avoided, either because creditors are determined to bankrupt those who owe them money, or because debtors have found it impossible to reach agreement with creditors. In such cases bankruptcy will ensue.

There are three ways to go bankrupt. A creditor owed at least £750 can bring a petition against a person owing them that money, or a debtor can bring a petition against himself. The supervisor of an individual voluntary arrangement can also bankrupt a person involved if they fail to comply with the terms of the arrangement.

There are no restrictions on who can bankrupt themselves in England, Wales and Northern Ireland, although there are restrictions in Scotland. In Scotland, a debtor must have court judgements against him totalling £1,500 before he can bankrupt himself.

Creditor's petition

A creditor may bring a bankruptcy petition against anyone who owes them £750 or more (as of April 2002), or two or more creditors may combine together, as long as the total debts equal that amount. The normal procedure is that a creditor must serve a statutory demand on the debtor, demanding payment of the debt within three weeks. If the debt is not paid within this time, then the creditor can proceed to issue a bankruptcy petition against the debtor.

Debtor's petition

A debtor can bring their own bankruptcy petition by obtaining a bankruptcy petition form from their local county court (the High Court in the Strand for those living within the London insolvency district). On completion of this form, which lists debts, assets and other information, a telephone call to the court should be made, to arrange an appointment for a bankruptcy hearing. The completed form is then taken to the court with the necessary fee in cash (this is £377 for an individual as at April 2002). The current fee can found by asking the relevant court. A bankruptcy order will usually be made immediately, on presentation of the fee and the petition. This is the position in all the countries of the UK except Scotland. In Scotland, debtors need to obtain petition forms from their nearest Sheriff's court.

The immediate aftermath of a bankruptcy order

Once a bankruptcy order has been made, then all the assets and property of the bankrupt person vest with the official receiver (Accountant in Bankruptcy in Scotland) and that person's estate is then administered by the official receiver.

The official receiver is a civil servant employed by the Insolvency Service – a department of the DTI. It is his/her job to sell any assets that a bankrupt person my have and distribute the proceeds to their creditors. This process includes a bankrupt person's home. If there are assets in an estate e.g. a house to sell, then the case is often handed over to outside accountants who are called trustees in bankruptcy.

If debtors have brought a petition against themselves then they will normally speak to their official receiver from the court by telephone after the bankruptcy order has been made. The official receiver will ask for details of the bankrupt person's bank accounts and other information. The bankrupt is legally bound to answer such questions.

An appointment will then normally be arranged for the bankrupt to attend the official receiver's office for an interview. Depending on the information given by the bankrupt the official receiver may arrange for agents to visit the bankrupt's business address to immediately seize any assets. It is extremely rare for the official receiver to send anyone to a bankrupt's home address in England or Wales if they are not in business. In Scotland however, a home visit is always made to a bankrupt's home.

Bank accounts

The first step an official receiver will take will be to immediately freeze any bank or building society accounts in which a bankrupt person has an interest. This includes any joint accounts. In most cases any money is taken and distributed amongst the creditors. Consequently the accounts are subsequently closed leaving the bankrupt with no banking facilities.

Thus a husband and wife would not have access to any money in those accounts. Money belonging to a non-bankrupt spouse would be returned, but this takes time and will cause much inconvenience. It is vitally important for a non-bankrupt spouse to open their own bank account before the bankruptcy

Many bankrupt people find it extremely difficult to obtain new accounts. For example, it is virtually impossible for a bankrupt person to acquire a cheque guarantee card. In fact, strictly speaking, a bankrupt should not operate a current bank account without the permission of their official receiver or trustee. Even with such permission most banks will not allow that facility. Therefore many bankrupt people are left in the position where they can neither pay wages into an account, nor pay bills through the account.

There are solutions to this problem. Some bankrupts have their salaries paid into a relative's account. Others open building society savings accounts. This must be done after the bankruptcy, because all bank accounts or savings accounts operated by someone at the point of bankruptcy will be closed down. A bankrupt must never accrue savings as these can be seized by the official receiver or trustee in bankruptcy.

Obtaining future credit

It is a criminal offence for a bankrupt to obtain credit of more than £250 from any future creditor, without disclosing that he is a bankrupt. If a creditor is aware of the bankruptcy and offers credit of more than £250 then this is acceptable. Importantly, the bankrupt person must obtain the creditors written consent (evidence) if he is to avoid any possible legal repercussions.

Repercussions of bankruptcy

For anyone in debt, bankruptcy brings one huge overwhelming benefit. It frees them from pursuit by creditors. In due course they are released from these debts. It should be noted that a bankrupt is not freed from court fines, maintenance, or child support agency orders or from any debts that have arisen as a result of fraud.

Many bankrupt people loose their homes, their jobs, their livelihoods and until recently, they also lost their pensions. They have to live with a whole series of restrictions and difficulties throughout the period of a bankruptcy and beyond. Bankrupts are mainly honest people who have met with misfortune. Bankruptcy is therefore not an easy option.

This is just a brief outline of events that take place immediately after the making of a bankruptcy order. The sequence of these events may vary from area to area. In some areas the official receiver's office is close to the court and a debtor bringing his own petition might be sent around immediately to the official receiver's office.

The bankrupt's home

The official receiver owns a bankrupt person's share in any property – for life. Therefore unless the official receiver's interest in a property is legally purchased from them they are entitled to sell the family home at any time after one year. If another family member can raise the money to buy out the bankrupt's interest it can be bought from the official receiver or the trustee in bankruptcy.

Income payments orders

A bankrupt person is entitled to earn sufficient money to cover all reasonable living expenses. If there is a surplus income after all these expenses are met then the bankrupt is expected to pay a portion of any surplus to their official receiver or trustee in bankruptcy. If there is a dispute, the official receiver or trustee in bankruptcy can apply to the court to make an income payments order. The court will decide how much the bankrupt must pay. If this amount is not paid, without good reason, imprisonment may follow.

Council tax

If adult people are living together in a property and one goes bankrupt, then the other adult/s are liable for the current council tax that may be outstanding, although the bankrupt person is not. The bankrupt, however, is liable for future council tax from the date of the bankruptcy.

Pension rights

Pension rights in bankruptcy have been a sorely contested and much argued point in the past and many pension rights were lost. The Bankruptcy Association has campaigned against this injustice for many years. Thanks to pressure from the Bankruptcy Association and others the law was changed in June 2000. All pension rights for anyone presented with a bankruptcy petition after that date are protected.

Exempt property

Certain property is exempt from bankruptcy proceedings and it is worth quoting the precise letter of the law because, over the years, we have come across many instances where official receivers and trustees have overstepped the law and seized exempt property. The appropriate legal reference is section 283 of the Insolvency Act 1986. This section states that all property vests in the trustee except for:

'such tools, books, vehicles, and other items of equipment as are necessary to the bankrupt for use personally by him in his employment, business, or vocation'. (section 283 subsection 2(a))

'such clothing, bedding, furniture, household equipment and provisions as are necessary for satisfying the basic domestic needs of the bankrupt and his family'. (section 283 subsection 2(b))

The rule of thumb applied by the authorities is that they will allow a bankrupt to keep any particular item referred to above that is worth less than £500. Therefore a car worth more than £500 would be seized, as would a piece of antique furniture worth thousands of pounds. An ordinary person living in a typical semi-detached home with household equipment of normal value would be left with everything intact. Likewise a builder or photographer, or anyone else running a business, should be left with all items of equipment and vehicles worth less than £500 each.

Discharge from a first bankruptcy

An automatic discharge from a first bankruptcy is normally granted after three years. The discharge would only be suspended if the bankrupt had not co-operated with the proceedings or had broken the bankruptcy laws. If an official receiver or trustee wishes to suspend discharge and keep someone in bankruptcy, then he must make an application to the court, before the automatic discharge date. The bankrupt would be informed of this application and it would then be the decision of the court, on hearing the evidence, to make such order as it thinks fit.

If a bankrupt brought the bankruptcy petition against himself and, in addition, had debts of less than £20,000, he would receive an automatic discharge after two years.

A certificate of discharge may be obtained from the court in which a person was made bankrupt. Currently such a certificate costs £50 (as at April 2002). Legally there is no need to have such a certificate, as discharge is automatic.

Scotland

The costs for a debtor to bring a bankruptcy petition in Scotland and/or to obtain a certificate of discharge are currently much less than in the rest of the United Kingdom.

Epilogue

I was offering some advice to a member of the Bankruptcy Association on the telephone recently when he interrupted me to ask if he could say something. I stopped talking and he said to me: 'I would like to tell you why it is so good to be a member of the Association. Your newsletters and your books are all great, and the sensible advice you offer is great too. But the best part of all is being able to phone someone up and not be made to feel like a leper'.

When I finished that conversation I turned to my son and told him what had been said and commented that in many ways it was the nicest compliment I had ever received. But there is a sad side to that compliment paid to me because it shows that this person must have been meeting with negative attitudes everywhere else in society generally.

Money rules

We live in a society that is increasingly mirroring the sore of society that America has – one of money worship. We too in this country are heading the same way, measuring each other by our money wealth alone.

You cannot therefore be lower down the social order than to be a bankrupt and without money. The fact that such a person might have made massive contributions to society, by employing people in their business or working hard as a nurse or teacher for many years is irrelevant. If you have no money in our society you are treated as a nobody.

I find this harsh fact of modern society very depressing because I was brought up to respect and value other people by examining their personalities and strength of character – not on how much cash they may have in the bank.

The insolvency industry

It is particularly galling for those people without money to find themselves caught up in a world of extremely highly paid insolvency practitioners who have a great feast on their 'financial' carcasses. Insolvency practitioners are some of the highest paid professionals in Britain. Their fees have to come from somewhere. Many people have lost their homes merely to feed these huge salaries. It is a fact that creditors rarely receive dividends from a bankruptcy. In most cases ALL the money raised is paid in fees.

The government cares not a jot

During what is now twenty years of campaigning on this subject I have come across only one Member of Parliament with any interest in this subject across several parliaments. He is Austin Mitchell, MP for Grimsby and he has been raising his voice for many years in Parliament about the many abuses endemic in the world of insolvency.

Unfortunately, the House of Commons as a whole and the government generally care not a jot for people with money trouble. I think the government find the subject embarrassing particularly when most of these people are busy lining their own pockets. This is a sad but true fact of life.

Planned reforms of little help

I have criticised the government plans to reform our bankruptcy legislation. I thought that these reforms were so badly thought out that I hoped and expected them to be dropped. Unfortunately, these reforms will definitely take place.

The planned reforms form just a small part of a huge Enterprise Initiative, which, from a read of the proposals, generally looks to be the biggest waste of public money since they built the Millennium Dome.

As part of this package bankruptcy reforms are being hustled through without any independent review of the law having taken place. There has been a cursory consultation – really a fake one, where anyone who opposed the reforms was ignored. This is an insult to a modern democracy.

The most alarming proposal of all is that the Insolvency Service intends to and will join in the multi-million pound rip-off industry of individual and company voluntary arrangements by themselves setting up post-bankruptcy voluntary arrangements. This is not only disgraceful and an insult to the people of Britain – it is absolutely crackpot.

But we are back to the power of money again. Planned protection for the family homes of bankrupts have already been dropped, presumably because the insolvency profession do not want to see a drop in their take or that creditor organisations simply want to see people punished in this way if they go bankrupt.

The Insolvency Service based this decision on the views of one – and only one – bankrupt individual, despite the fact that well over one hundred members of the Bankruptcy Association voiced their support for a protection on the family home in person to the then head of the Insolvency Service – Peter Joyce – at a televised meeting at Reading University. This is in addition to the tens of thousands of people who have been able to personally express their disgust through the Bankruptcy Association at the lack of protection for the family home. In fact, this has been the main campaigning issue of the Bankruptcy Association for decades as it is the loss of the family home that causes the greatest distress, worry and hardship for people and their families in bankruptcy. This support has simply been ignored.

People in debt walk a hard road. Through the Association many people do not walk it alone. Whether the law is changed for the better or worse the Bankruptcy Association will continue to support people in debt and bankruptcy as it has done since 1983.

FURTHER PUBLICATIONS OF
THE BANKRUPTCY ASSOCIATION

BOOKS

BANKRUPTCY EXPLAINED: The Bankruptcy Association's Practical Guide to UK Insolvency Laws (Paperback)

This is the Bankruptcy Association's main guide to bankruptcy law. It details in layman's terms the basic workings of bankruptcy law in every country of the United Kingdom. It answers most of the questions that members have asked John McQueen over many years.

£7.95

BOOM TO BUST: The Great 1990s Slump (Hardback)

John McQueen founder of the Bankruptcy Association lived through the great slump of the 1990s in a special way. He was uniquely placed in the centre of it. In this book John McQueen turns a machine gun on the bankruptcy laws of the United Kingdom, as well as detailing the moving story of human suffering he lived through. He exposes, in the passing, many other flaws in the political and legal systems.

£12.95

SPECIALIST PUBLICATIONS

HOW TO SETTLE DEBTS WITH CREDITORS
A Bankruptcy Association Guide

This guide is designed to be a guide to settling debts with creditors. It offers a proven system to apply to both business and consumer debt problems that the Bankruptcy Association has applied successfully over many years. By using the guidance offered in this booklet many people will find that they themselves can deal with what they thought were overwhelming debt problems.

£9.95

SAVING THE FAMILY HOME IN BANKRUPTCY A Bankruptcy Association Guide

Saving the family home from an Official Receiver can be the single most important aspect of being bankrupt. There is scant information available on the subject. This guide outlines the process and details how to conduct such negotiations.

£9.95

CHOOSING THE CORRECT LEGAL FORMAT FOR RUNNING A BUSINESS

In this guide John McQueen details the legal formats available to entrepreneurs running a business. How to choose and set up the correct legal business format is explained, as is the importance of using the protection that the correct format can provide.

£9.95

BANKRUPTCY: THE REALITY

In this guide members of the Bankruptcy Association draw a complete picture of the realities of the world of bankruptcy. The stories related provide a fascinating insight into the experiences of bankrupt people. They also show the urgent need for unprejudiced reform of our bankruptcy laws. This is an important social document with its accounts of real life traumas.

£9.95

BOOK ORDER FORM

NAME:...

ADDRESS:...

....

....

PLEASE INDICATE THE BOOKS/BOOKLETS REQUIRED. ORDERS WILL BE SUPPLIED BY RETURN OF POST. THEY ARE ALL SENT POST FREE. ALTERNATIVELY ANY OF THE PUBLICATIONS BELOW CAN BE ORDERED THROUGH ANY GOOD BOOKSHOP.

TITLE	NO OF COPIES	PRICE	TOTAL
Bankruptcy Explained		£ 7.95	
How to Settle Debts with Creditors		£ 9.95	
Saving the Family Home in Bankruptcy		£ 9.95	
Choosing the Correct Legal Format for Running a Business		£ 9.95	
Bankruptcy: The Reality		£ 9.95	
Boom to Bust		£12.95	
Total Enclosed		£	

PAYMENT CAN BE MADE EITHER BY CASH, CHEQUE OR POSTAL ORDER. MAKE CHEQUES PAYABLE TO EITHER 'THE BANKRUPTCY ASSOCIATION' OR 'JOHN MCQUEEN' AND SEND WITH YOUR COMPLETED FORM TO:

THE BANKRUPTCY ASSOCIATION
FREEPOST
4 JOHNSON CLOSE
LANCASTER
LA1 1BR